Since the dawn of time, people and animals have worked together, played together and kept each other company. Saints throughout the ages have loved their animal friends and, in return, the beasts have loved them back. We hope you enjoy this sampling of stories that reveals the compassion, respect and affection holy people have shown for all of God's creatures.

For Father Doug Lorig, who has the ability to see the fingerprints of God throughout all creation. And for the late Monsignor Michael Nestor, who always cherished the many charmed moments with his four-legged friend, Shadow.

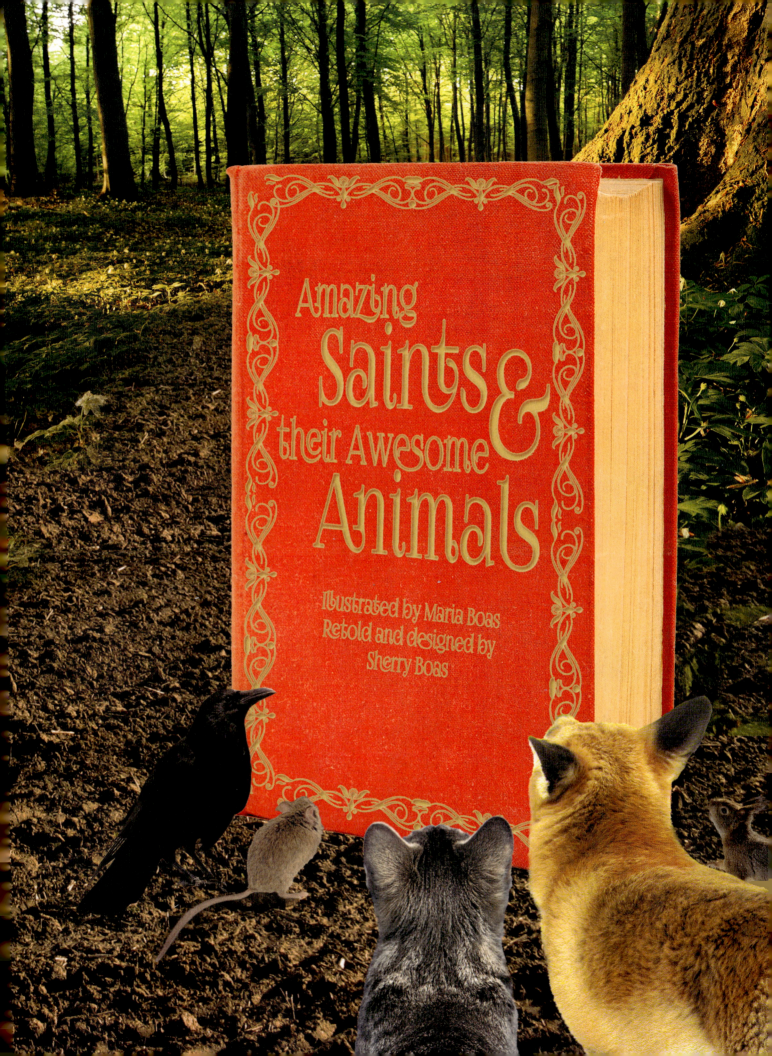

The people of Gubio, Italy, where Francis was staying, were petrified of a wolf who was terrorizing the town. The ravenous animal not only hunted down livestock, but killed the townspeople as well. The men who had gone out into the wilderness to find and kill the wolf had fallen victim to the animal. People were afraid to leave the walls of their city. Moved with pity, Francis decided to go out to meet the wolf. Ignoring everyone's warnings, Francis assured the people that God would protect him, and the brave saint set out into the wilderness.

Upon seeing Francis, the wolf began to close in on him. Francis made the sign of the cross, and commanded, "Come to me, Brother Wolf. In the name of Christ, I order you not to hurt anyone."

With an uncanny ability to communicate with animals, Francis learned from the wolf that he had been injured and left behind by his pack and had no choice but to attack slow-moving livestock, though he would have preferred deer. He only killed the men to defend his life. Francis explained to the wolf how much pain and suffering he had caused the people, and the wolf became remorseful.

Francis made a pact with the wolf never to hurt anyone again if the people would bring him food. Francis put out his hand, and the wolf laid his paw in Francis' hand to signify he agreed to the terms. The wolf and the people of 13th-Century Gubio became friends and remained allies ever after. St. Francis' feast day is October 4.

Donkey

Anthony was a gifted 13th-Century preacher who was very devoted to Jesus truly present in the Holy Eucharist. One day, the Lisbon-born brother met a man who did not believe the consecrated bread we receive at Mass is the true body of Christ. Anthony made a bet with the man that even his donkey would recognize and adore Jesus in the Blessed Sacrament. So the man agreed to bring his donkey back to carry out the bet. The man planned to also bring hay with him to distract the donkey. To make sure the donkey was good and hungry, the man did not feed his animal for three days. Because the man had told everyone about the bet, a great crowd gathered as the animal was led to where St. Anthony was standing, holding the Blessed Sacrament. Just before reaching Anthony, the man placed a bag of hay right under the hungry donkey's nose. The donkey ignored the hay and fell down on his on knees before Jesus in the Blessed Sacrament. St. Anthony's feast day is June 13.

Fox

Once, in 5th-Century Ireland, a king had a beloved pet fox. He had tamed the once-wild animal and trained it to perform all kinds of tricks. One day, a hunter mistook the King's fox for a wild animal and killed it. The distraught king sentenced the man to death and his family to slavery unless the fox could be replaced by one just as tame. Hearing of the tragic story, Bridget jumped in her chariot and set out for the king's court to see if there might be some way to save the man and his family. On the way there, a fox jumped into the chariot and nestled into Bridget's clothes. She took the animal to the king, who was delighted to see the fox was just as tame and clever as the one who had been killed. The king spared the hunter's life and let his family go free. St. Bridget's feast day is February 1.

Saint Benedict

Saint Benedict, a 6th-Century monk from Nursia, Italy, had a raven friend whom he frequently shared his bread with. One day, a priest who was jealous of Benedict's holiness sent him a loaf of bread that was tainted with poison. Benedict knew the bread was poisoned and told the raven to dispose of it.

"In the name of Jesus Christ our Lord, take up that loaf, and leave it in some such place where no man may find it." The raven opened his mouth, spread his wings, cawed and began hopping up and down, trying to tell the monk that he wanted to obey him, but could not accomplish what he'd been asked to do.

Benedict insisted, telling his winged friend again and again, "Take it up without fear, and throw it where no man may find it." Finally, the raven took the bread in its beak and flew away. Three hours later, the bird returned, and Benedict gave him his usual helping of bread from his table. St. Benedict's feast day is July 11.

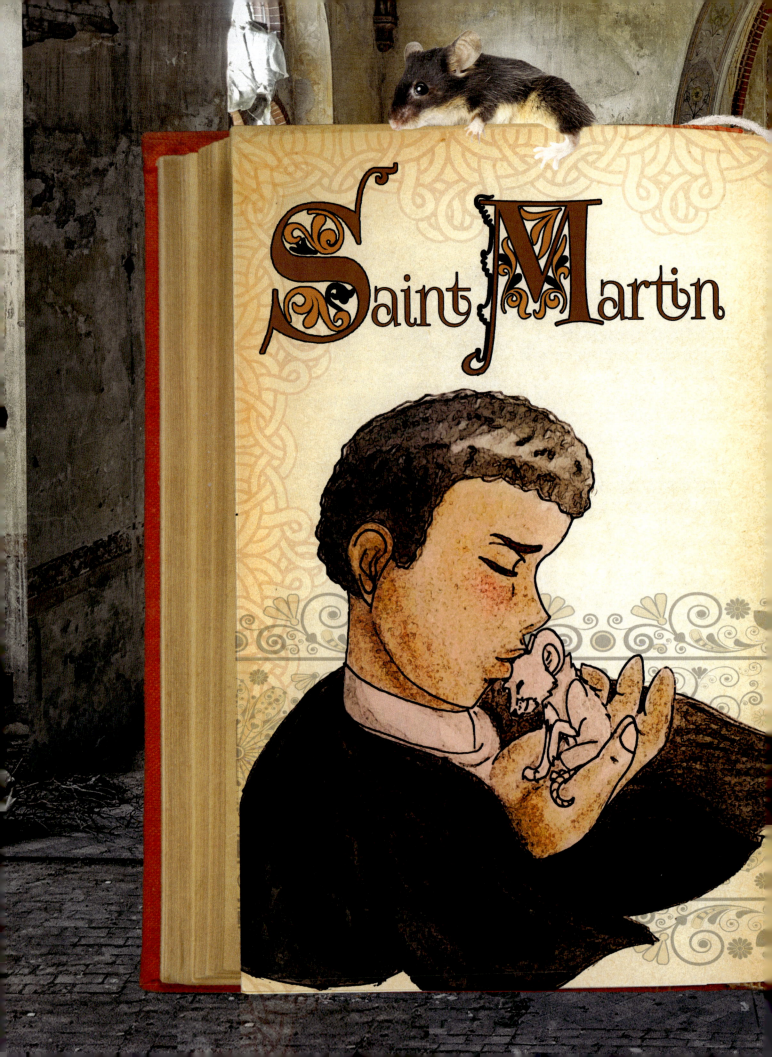

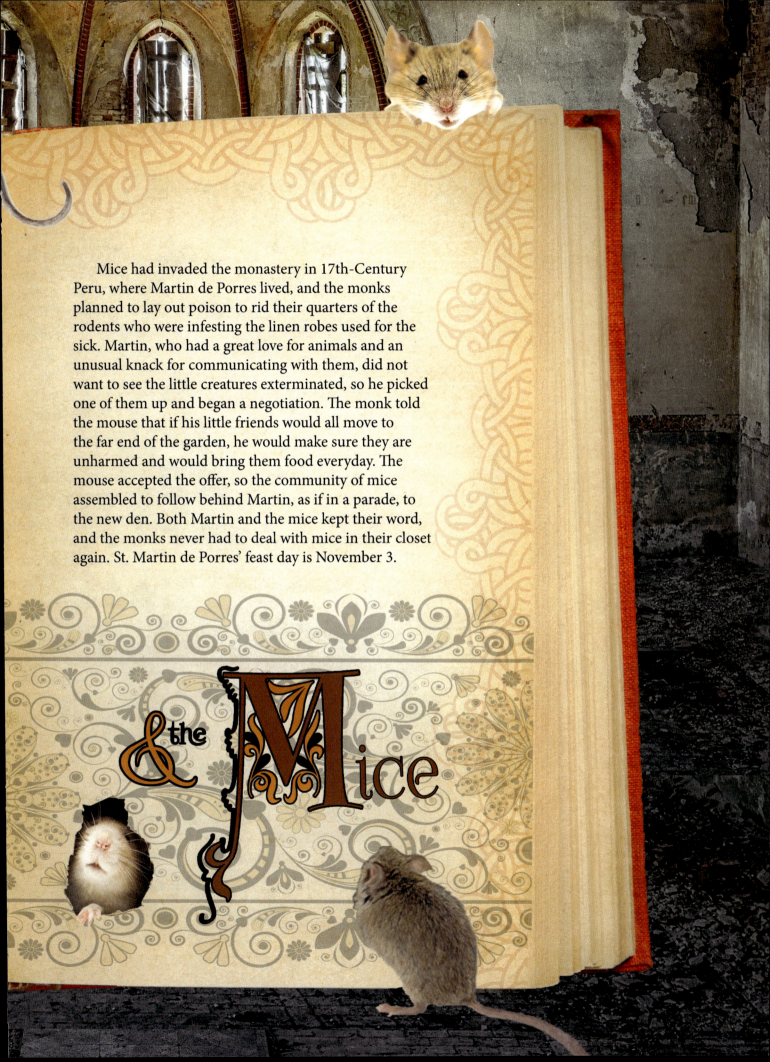

Mice had invaded the monastery in 17th-Century Peru, where Martin de Porres lived, and the monks planned to lay out poison to rid their quarters of the rodents who were infesting the linen robes used for the sick. Martin, who had a great love for animals and an unusual knack for communicating with them, did not want to see the little creatures exterminated, so he picked one of them up and began a negotiation. The monk told the mouse that if his little friends would all move to the far end of the garden, he would make sure they are unharmed and would bring them food everyday. The mouse accepted the offer, so the community of mice assembled to follow behind Martin, as if in a parade, to the new den. Both Martin and the mice kept their word, and the monks never had to deal with mice in their closet again. St. Martin de Porres' feast day is November 3.

& the Mice

On his last day on earth, something amazing happened to St. Columba, the 6th-Century founder of a monastery on the island of Iona, off the Western Coast of Scotland. He had spent his life traveling the countryside and preaching. Knowing that he was going to die that day, Columba went out into the fields where his brother monks were working so he could say good-bye. There was much sorrow at the news. He headed back toward the monastery, but had to stop and rest along the side of the road since he was so weak. Columba's work horse ran to him, pushed his nuzzle into the priest's chest, and wept bitterly, drenching the monk's garment with his tears. A fellow monk tried to remove the animal, but Columba told him to let his faithful companion be. The horse instinctively knew that he would not see his human friend again after that day. Columba blessed the horse, and the animal went on his way. Later that night, when the bell tolled for midnight service, Columba made his way into the monastery church and collapsed at the Holy Altar, breathing his last at the age of 77.

St. Columba's feast day is June 9.

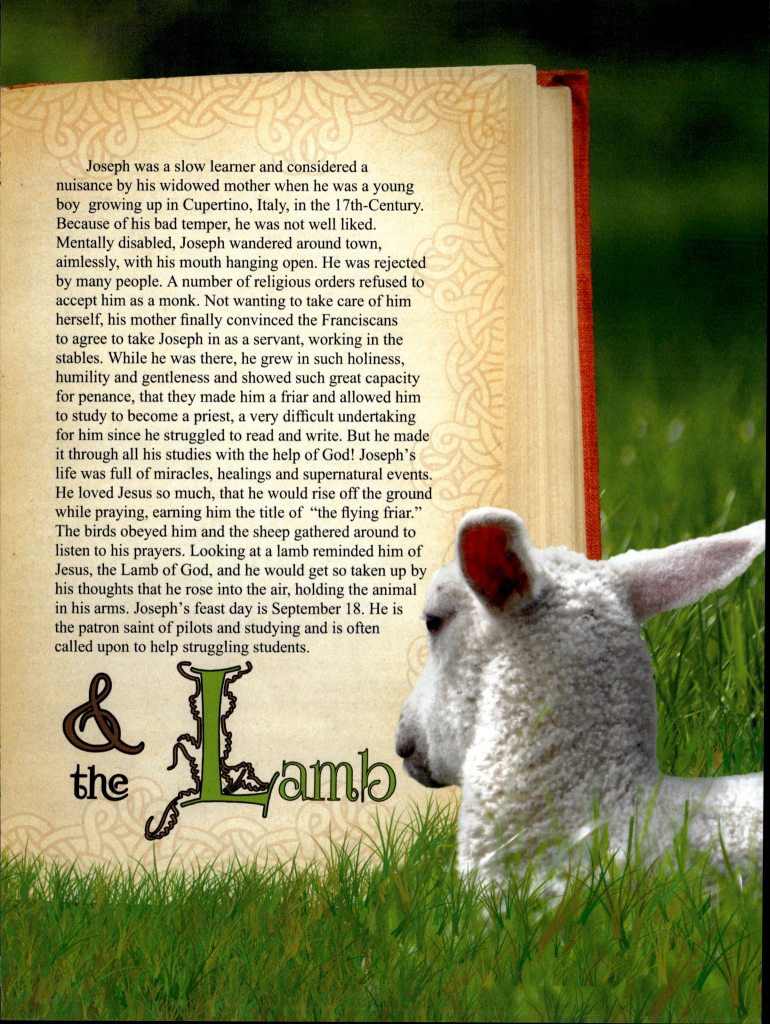

Joseph was a slow learner and considered a nuisance by his widowed mother when he was a young boy growing up in Cupertino, Italy, in the 17th-Century. Because of his bad temper, he was not well liked. Mentally disabled, Joseph wandered around town, aimlessly, with his mouth hanging open. He was rejected by many people. A number of religious orders refused to accept him as a monk. Not wanting to take care of him herself, his mother finally convinced the Franciscans to agree to take Joseph in as a servant, working in the stables. While he was there, he grew in such holiness, humility and gentleness and showed such great capacity for penance, that they made him a friar and allowed him to study to become a priest, a very difficult undertaking for him since he struggled to read and write. But he made it through all his studies with the help of God! Joseph's life was full of miracles, healings and supernatural events. He loved Jesus so much, that he would rise off the ground while praying, earning him the title of "the flying friar." The birds obeyed him and the sheep gathered around to listen to his prayers. Looking at a lamb reminded him of Jesus, the Lamb of God, and he would get so taken up by his thoughts that he rose into the air, holding the animal in his arms. Joseph's feast day is September 18. He is the patron saint of pilots and studying and is often called upon to help struggling students.

& the Lamb

St. Gall, a 7th-Century Irish monk, was travelling in the woods in Switzerland when a hungry bear charged him. Gall, also called Gallen, had little bread, but shared it with the bear. The bear was so affected by the monk's holiness, the animal became calm and docile and retrieved wood to feed the fire by which Gall warmed his hands.

Legend says the bear followed Gall wherever he went after that. Today, the city of St. Gallen, Switzerland, pays tribute to the saint. The bear is on the city's coat of arms and can be seen on signs throughout the historic district, where the Abbey of St. Gall still stands in the heart of the city. A football team in Switzerland took the name, *The St. Gallen Bears*.
St. Gall's feast day is October 16.

Giles was born into a wealthy family in Greece, and his parents left him a great deal of money when they died. Giles used his riches to help people in need. Because of this, and because he worked many miracles, Giles became very popular. He did not want all the praise to make him proud, so he set sail for France to live alone in a cave, where he happily spent his days praying. God sent him a deer who provided him with milk.

One day the king and his men were out hunting in the woods when they spotted the deer, who escaped into the cave that was hidden behind a thorn bush. The hunters shot into the bush, and the arrow entered the cave and hit Giles. The king found Giles wounded and asked who he was and why he was living in the cave. Upon hearing Giles' story, the king begged forgiveness and sent doctors to care for him. The king was so impressed with Giles that he visited him often, bearing gifts which Giles refused to accept. Finally the king convinced Giles to let him build a large monastery, and Giles became its first abbot. The monastery gained such fame that people wanted to live near it, and a town grew up around it. Many of the townsfolk ended up becoming monks.

St. Giles' feast day is September 1.

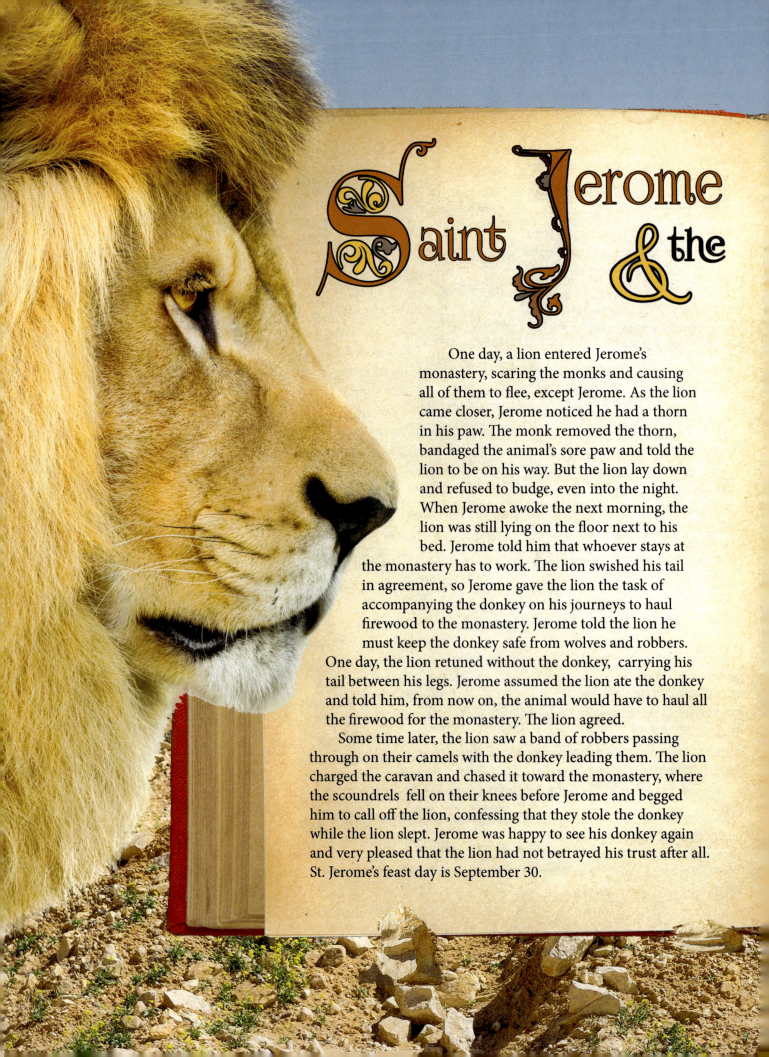

Saint Jerome & the

One day, a lion entered Jerome's monastery, scaring the monks and causing all of them to flee, except Jerome. As the lion came closer, Jerome noticed he had a thorn in his paw. The monk removed the thorn, bandaged the animal's sore paw and told the lion to be on his way. But the lion lay down and refused to budge, even into the night. When Jerome awoke the next morning, the lion was still lying on the floor next to his bed. Jerome told him that whoever stays at the monastery has to work. The lion swished his tail in agreement, so Jerome gave the lion the task of accompanying the donkey on his journeys to haul firewood to the monastery. Jerome told the lion he must keep the donkey safe from wolves and robbers. One day, the lion retuned without the donkey, carrying his tail between his legs. Jerome assumed the lion ate the donkey and told him, from now on, the animal would have to haul all the firewood for the monastery. The lion agreed.

Some time later, the lion saw a band of robbers passing through on their camels with the donkey leading them. The lion charged the caravan and chased it toward the monastery, where the scoundrels fell on their knees before Jerome and begged him to call off the lion, confessing that they stole the donkey while the lion slept. Jerome was happy to see his donkey again and very pleased that the lion had not betrayed his trust after all. St. Jerome's feast day is September 30.

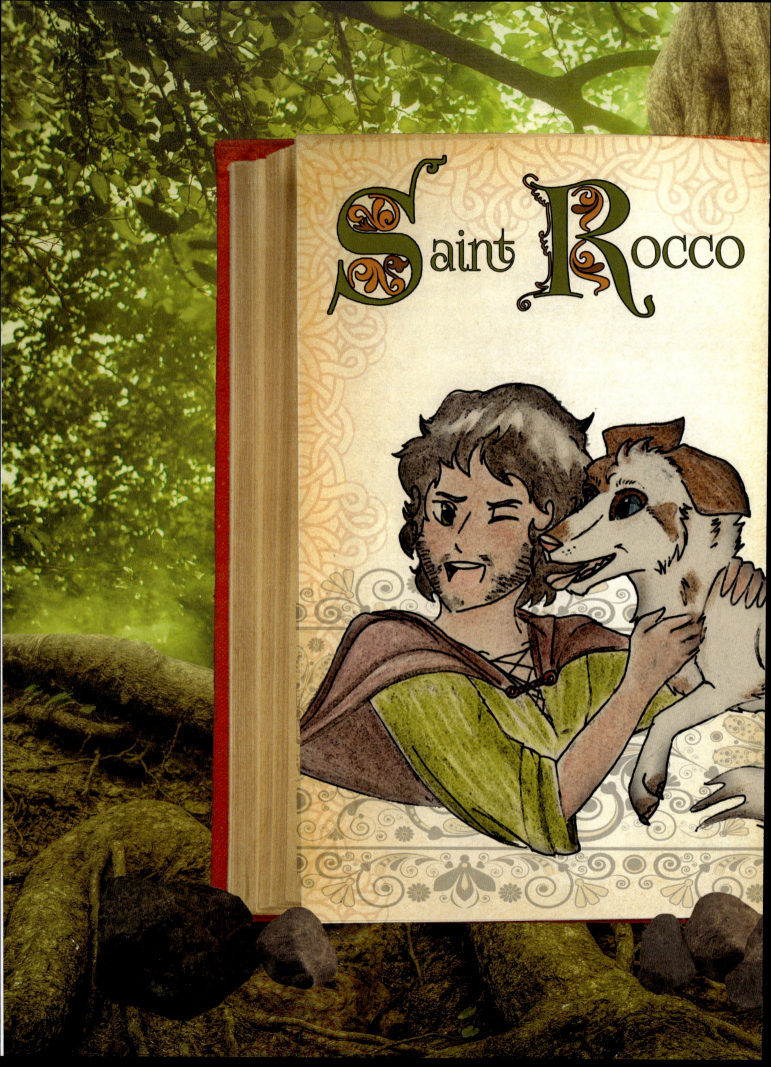

& the Dog

St. Rocco lived in 14th-Century Italy during the time of a horrible plague. He cured people by making the sign of the cross and praying for them. Eventually, he too was stricken with the dreadful disease, which caused an open sore on his leg. Because the disease was contagious, Rocco was not allowed to be around anyone else. He lived in a cave outside the city and drank from a stream. A dog brought him bread so he would not starve. One day, the owner of the dog, a nobleman, followed to see where his pet was going with the bread. He found Rocco in the woods and took him back to his castle to care for him until he was cured. St. Rocco's feast day is August 16.

& the Bees

Modomnoc was a beekeeper who was assigned to take care of the honey bees in the monastery garden, where he lived in 6th-Century Wales. He planted all kinds of flowers that bees love. As he worked, clouds of bees buzzed around him, and he talked to them. The other monks were afraid to go in the corner of the garden where the bees were kept, but Modomnoc considered the bees his friends, and they never stung him. When his studies to become a priest were over, and he was to return to Ireland to begin his priestly vocation, Modomnoc said goodbye to his human and bee friends at the monastery and set sail for Ireland. When the ship had traveled three miles, Modomnoc looked out across the sea and noticed a large black cloud approaching. The bees were following him! He took them back to Wales and tried to leave again the following day, but again, they followed. When the same thing happened a third time, the abbot told Modomnoc to take the bees with him and give them a new home in Ireland, since it was apparent they didn't want to live without him. Upon arriving in Ireland, he built a Church in Bremore, which is to this day, called "the beekeeper's church" (Llan-Beach-Aire). Modomnoc's winged friends settled into their new homes in beehives he built in a garden near the church. It is said that this is how honey bees and beekeeping were first introduced to Ireland. Modomonoc is the patron saint of bees and beekeepers. His feast day is February 13.

Hugh, a 12th-Century monk who craved peace and quiet, loved to spend his time with the birds and other wildlife at the lake near Lincoln, England. When he was elected Bishop, a very large and cranky swan appeared on the lake and drove off all the other wildlife. The swan was captured and presented to the new Bishop, who fed it bread and immediately won it over. The swan never left Hugh's side, but when the Bishop had to leave the lake to attend to business, the swan would return to his former ways of terrorizing people and animals. On the Bishop's return, the swan would jealously guard and protect him like a watchdog, and only relented when the Bishop called him off. One time, Hugh had to be away for two years, but the swan still remembered him when he returned, stretching out its wings to greet him and then following him into his house, where it shared daily in the bishop's bread. After knowing each other for fifteen years, the swan became sad just before the Bishop's death. The swan lived for several more years, but never had another friend. St. Hugh's feast day is November 17.

Blessed Maria

Maria Bagnesi was sick all her life and spent a great deal of time in bed. She had visions and talked to angels and saints. She was so holy, many people in her 16th-Century town of Florence, Italy, would come to her room to be in her presence, seeking her wisdom and finding comfort in the peace that surrounded her.

Animals liked to be with Maria as well. Cats really loved her, and you could find many sleeping in her room, lounging on her bed and even guarding her pet songbirds. There is a story that, when Maria was hungry, one of the cats set out in search of some cheese and brought it to her.

A Dominican tertiary, Maria spent her entire life in Florence, dying at the age of 62 after bouts of pleurisy, asthma and kidney disease. Her feast day is May 27.

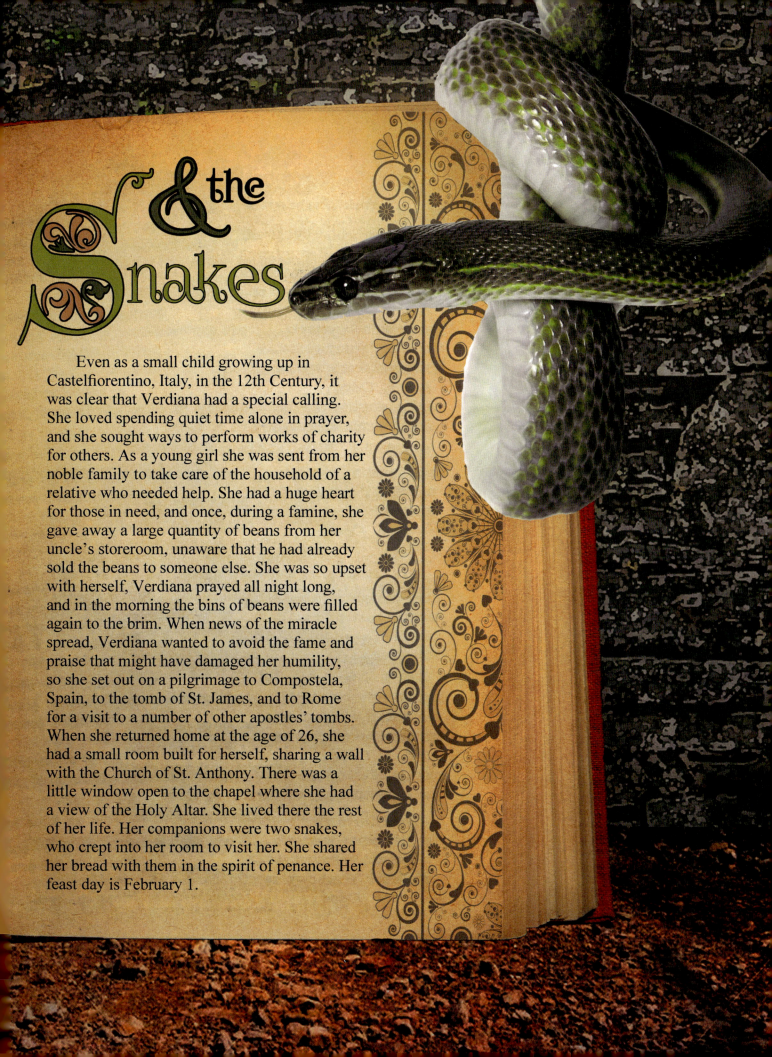

V & the Snakes

Even as a small child growing up in Castelfiorentino, Italy, in the 12th Century, it was clear that Verdiana had a special calling. She loved spending quiet time alone in prayer, and she sought ways to perform works of charity for others. As a young girl she was sent from her noble family to take care of the household of a relative who needed help. She had a huge heart for those in need, and once, during a famine, she gave away a large quantity of beans from her uncle's storeroom, unaware that he had already sold the beans to someone else. She was so upset with herself, Verdiana prayed all night long, and in the morning the bins of beans were filled again to the brim. When news of the miracle spread, Verdiana wanted to avoid the fame and praise that might have damaged her humility, so she set out on a pilgrimage to Compostela, Spain, to the tomb of St. James, and to Rome for a visit to a number of other apostles' tombs. When she returned home at the age of 26, she had a small room built for herself, sharing a wall with the Church of St. Anthony. There was a little window open to the chapel where she had a view of the Holy Altar. She lived there the rest of her life. Her companions were two snakes, who crept into her room to visit her. She shared her bread with them in the spirit of penance. Her feast day is February 1.

Blaise cared so deeply for every living thing that he studied medicine so he could help heal people and animals in his village in 4th-Century Turkey. He had a gift for taming wild animals. All the birds, mammals and fish loved him because he never harmed them and did all he could to help them recover if they were ill or injured.

One day, a cruel governor sent his soldiers into the wilderness to gather ferocious animals who would be released into a large arena to kill Christians in front of a cheering crowd. The soldiers searched and searched and, strangely, found no wild animals. They happened upon a cave where St. Blaise lived, and there they found all the lions, tigers, leopards, bears and wolves, sitting peacefully, waiting for Blaise to finish his morning prayers so they could pay him a visit. Although the animals were scared of the soldiers' spears and nets, they sat perfectly still and did not make a sound because they did not want to disturb Blaise's prayers. They just glared fiercely at the soldiers, who were so bewildered at the animals' behavior, they fled back into the city. St. Blaise's feast day is February 3.

Prayer of Saint Francis for Animals

God Our Heavenly Father,
You created the world
to serve humanity's needs
and to lead them to You.
By our own fault
we have lost the beautiful relationship
which we once had with all your creation.
Help us to see
that by restoring our relationship with You
we will also restore it
with all Your creation.
Give us the grace
to see all animals as gifts from You
and to treat them with respect
for they are Your creation.

We pray for all animals
who are suffering as a result of our neglect.
May the order You originally established
be once again restored to the whole world
through the intercession of the Glorious
Virgin Mary,
the prayers of Saint Francis
and the merits of Your Son,
Our Lord Jesus Christ
Who lives and reigns with You
now and forever. Amen.

About the Author and Illustrator

Sherry Boas cherishes her childhood memories of long, lingering days, walking her Spaniel in the New England woods, peering at song birds through binoculars, watching squirrels scurry away with the mixed nuts her mom put out on the redwood deck, and later, going inside for a game of "animals talk" with her plush toys and best friend, who happened to live next door. Now, Boas writes books about animals and other stuff. Though she misses the towering trees and boundless imagination of youth, she finds her work as a Catholic author just as much fun as playing "animals talk."

Maria Boas has been drawing since she was three years old, when she became inspired to draw horses by watching the movie *Spirit: Stallion of the Cimarron*. She drew forty horses a day for the next seven years, and then decided to try her hand at other animals, mostly wolves. Maria hopes to pursue a career in film, while continuing to produce artwork that glorifies God. The home school graduate looks forward to many new college adventures and a life brimming with both human and animal friends.

Other children's books available from
CaritasPress.org and CatholicWord.com

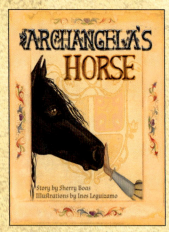
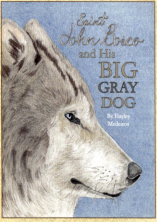
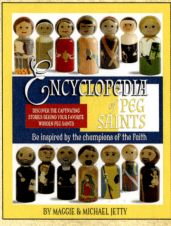
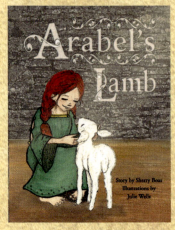

ARCHANGELA'S HORSE
Archangela comes to understand God's will when her beloved and loyal horse refuses to take her where she wants to go. By Sherry Boas

SAINT JOHN BOSCO AND HIS BIG GRAY DOG
Colorfully-illustrated story of a very special canine guardian who appeared out of nowhere to protect St. John Bosco whenever he was in danger. By Hayley Madieros

ENCYCLOPEDIA OF PEG SAINTS
Get to know 36 saints in an engaging and easy to "absorb" format, centered around colorful hand-painted peg dolls collected and cherished by Catholic kids everywhere. By Maggie & Michael Jetty

ARABEL'S LAMB
A young girl's compassion is tested to the limits in this gripping tale about love and sacrifice. Loosely based on the legend of St. George and the Dragon. By Sherry Boas

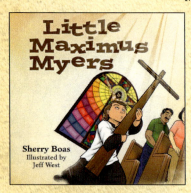
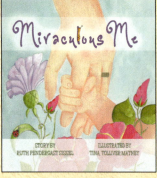
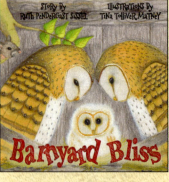
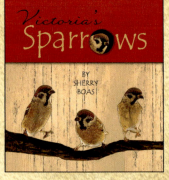

LITTLE MAXIMUS MYERS
Little Maximus Myers never liked being little, until one day, while carrying the cross in the procession at Mass, he discovered how our weaknesses can bring us closer to Christ. By Sherry Boas

MIRACULOUS ME
A mother and father dream of the future as they celebrate the precious gift of life, the baby who is about to arrive. What will the days of her life hold? By Ruth Pendergast Sissel & Tina Tolliver Matney

BARNYARD BLISS
All of creation rejoices as word of the baby owlet spreads throughout the farm from one animal to the next. By Ruth Pendergast Sissel & Tina Tolliver Matney

VICTORIA'S SPARROWS
A young girl sees God's providence at work after her day takes a turn she didn't expect. By Sherry Boas

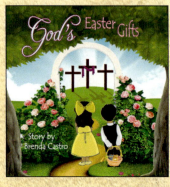
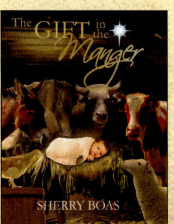

THE GIFT IN THE MANGER
When their feeding trough ends up serving as a bed for a tiny baby, the animals get a glimpse into God's loving plan to save the world. Like every one of us, each of the animals gathered around the manger has a struggle to overcome. They, like us, find the answer in Jesus, the only one who can fix our brokenness, heal our imperfections and give us the gift that makes us whole – the gift of Himself. By Sherry Boas

BILLOWTAIL
Little creatures on a big adventure in medieval Spain! 220-page Novel. By Sherry Boas

GOD'S EASTER GIFTS
A very special Easter egg hunt shows brother and sister, Pablo and Bella, that there's much more to Easter than candy and toys. By Brenda Castro

That wondrous night seen through the eyes of the animals. Baby Jesus' future is foretold, and we see the much needed grace He brings to our lives.

Books for Mom & Dad

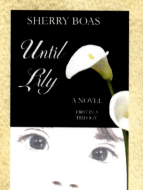
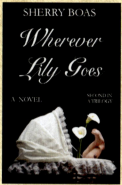
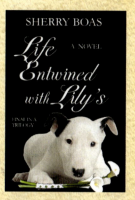

THE LILY SERIES BY SHERRY BOAS
Until Lily
Wherever Lily Goes
Life Entwined with Lily's
The Things Lily Knew
Things Unknown to Lily
A Little Like Lily

"...You will be entranced, you will experience the joys and sorrows of the characters, you will cry, and you will not be able to put Lily down."
– Dr. Jeff Mirus of CatholicCulture.org

The transforming power of love is at the heart of Sherry Boas' poignant series about the people whose lives are moved by a woman with Down syndrome. Lily's story is told with such brutal yet touching honesty, it will have you laughing one minute and reduced to tears the next.

WING TIP
A Novel

Dante De Luz's steel was forged in his youth, in the crucible of harsh losses and triumphant love. But that steel gets tested like never before as his mother's deathbed confession reveals something startling about his father and presents the young Catholic priest with the toughest challenge of his life, with stakes that couldn't get any higher.

"Aside from death and taxes, here's one more thing that is certain in this life: Sherry Boas' *Wing Tip*, will be a classic of Catholic literature. Magnificent read, highly recommended."

Robert Curtis,
The Catholic Sun

Rosary meditations for everyone in the family

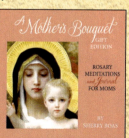

Dads • Moms • Children • Teens • Grandparents • Altar Servers • Special full-color **Gift Edition and Journal for Mom**

CaritasPress.org

Amazing Saints & their Awesome Animals
Copyright © 2016 Sherry Boas (text and design), Maria Boas (saint and animal artwork)
Printed in the USA

First Edition
10 9 8 7 6 5 4 3 2 1
ISBN 978-1-940209-26-5

No part of this publication may be reproduced, stored in a retrieval system or transmitted in any form or by any means, electronic, mechanical, photocopying, recording or otherwise without written permission of the publisher.

Contact Sherry@LilyTrilogy.com

Stock Images used in design purchased from Fotolia:

© BillionPhotos.com, © Yuriy Seleznyov, © keller, © taviphoto, © Eric Isselée, © johnsroad7, © Eric Isselée, © Farinoza, © Naj, © rima15, © lom742, © Štěpán Kápl, © Eric Isselée, © George Dolgikh, ©Rokfeler, © olllinka2, © JackF, © lexuss, © annaav, © Sondem, © M. Siegmund, © schankz, © swety76, © Mariusz Niedzwiedzki, © opel2b, © Kirsty Pargeter, © ansaharju, © DragoNika, © Alexandr Satoru, © determined, © Sergey Nivens, © kesipun, © chemie1964, © Olga Itina, © khlongwangchao, ©jamenpercy, © Mr Twister, © groster, © Alexander Potapov, © Eric Isselée, © iofoto, © Oksana Kuzmina, © Kseniya, © svetlana, © Alekss, © SM Web, © artyzan12, © Pavel Klimenko, © Alekss, ©George Dolgikh, © Kavita

CARITAS PRESS

CaritasPress.org

Caritas Press was founded in 2011 with the mission of shedding light on things eternal in a culture that is becoming increasingly blind to the wonders of God's works and numb to His boundless love. Making use of the subtle and the beautiful, Caritas Press hopes to play a part in igniting in children and adults a desire to know God more fully. For a full listing of all Caritas titles for children, youths and adults, visit CaritasPress.org.

Made in the USA
Monee, IL
27 March 2024

55907449R00026